PARENT PIANO METHOD

Empowering Parents To Give
The Gift of Music and Their Time

LEVEL 1
THEORY WORKBOOK

Classical Piano Lessons in Just 20 Minutes a Week!

By Stephanie Parker

Table Of Contents

Introduction:

This theory workbook is meant to be a supplement to the corresponding teaching book. Unlike the teaching book, which needs direct parent involvement, this theory book may function more independently. Coursework should be printed, assigned to your child, and then graded by you. If a student struggles to complete a theory page correctly, print it out again and let them rework it over and over until the concept is mastered before continuing to the next chapter. Music is designed to be repetitive in its teaching for a mastery of understanding. You may see exercises repeated. This is done purposefully and will give a stronger foundation to your child's comprehension of music.

CHAPTER 1: Learning the Basics

Stephanie Parker

LESSON 1

1. Color the Right hand BLUE and color the left hand RED

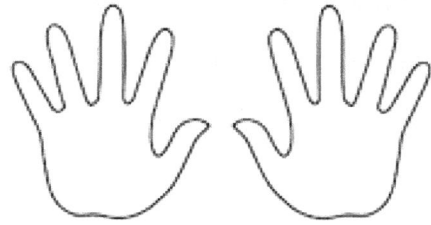

2. Write in the correct finger numbers above each finger in the left and right hand

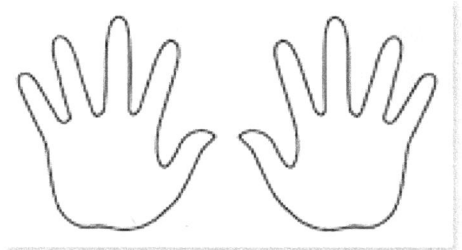

3. Color the low end of the piano BLUE and the high end of the piano RED

4. Circle all the groups of 2 black notes

5. Circle all the groups of 3 black notes

LESSON 2

1) Which finger number is the arrow pointing to on each RIGHT hand image.

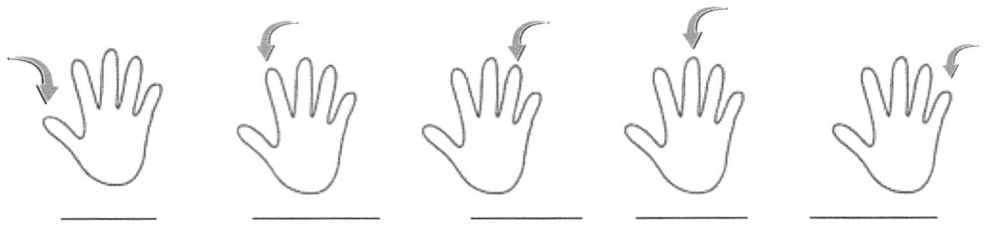

_____ _____ _____ _____ _____

2) Which finger number is the arrow point to on each LEFT hand image

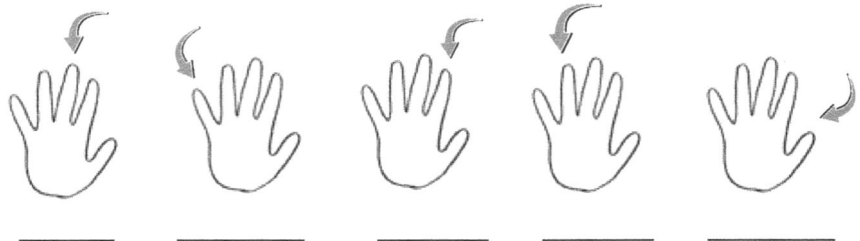

_____ _____ _____ _____ _____

3) Circle all the groups of 2 black notes

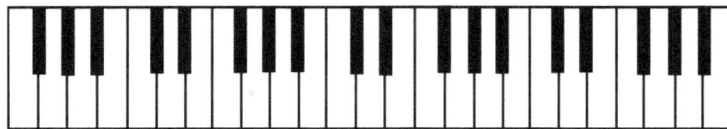

4) Color all The C's on the piano

5) Matching:

Quarter note   𝅗𝅥

Half note   𝅝

Whole note   𝅘𝅥

6) How many beats in a 𝅘𝅥 _____?

7) How many beats in a 𝅝 _____?

8) How many beats in a 𝅗𝅥 _____?

LESSON 3

1) Color all the C's on the piano

2) Color all the D's on the piano

3) Color all the E's on the piano

4) Color all the F's on the piano

5) Color all the G's on the piano

6) Color all the A's on the piano

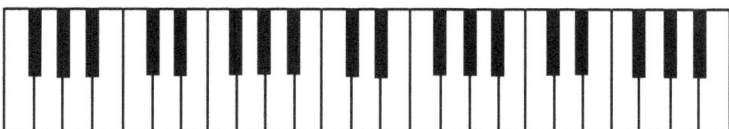

7) Color all the B's on the piano

LESSON 4

1) Are the notes going up or going down? _____

2) Are the notes going up or going down? _____

3) $\boldsymbol{p}$ stands for the word _____ and means to play _____.

4) $\boldsymbol{f}$ stands for the word _____ and means to play _____.

5) Color the D's red, the F's blue and the A's yellow.

6) Color the E's red, the G's blue and the B's yellow.

LESSON 5

1) Color the D's red, the F's blue and the A's yellow.

2) Color the E's red, the G's blue and the B's yellow.

3) Are the notes going up, down, or staying the same? _____

4) Are the notes going up, down, or staying the same? _____

5) Are the notes going up, down, or staying the same? _____

LESSON 6

1) Color the D's red, the F's blue and the A's yellow.

2) Color the E's red, the G's blue and the B's yellow.

3) Matching

Quarter note	𝅗𝅥
Piano	*f*
Whole note	♩
Forte	𝅝
Half note	*p*

CHAPTER 2: Lines, Spaces and Counting Music

LESSON 1

1) 　　　is called _____.

2) 　　　is called a _____.

3) *f*　　is called _____.

4) *p*　　is called _____.

5) 　　　is called a _____.

6) 　　　is called a _____.

7) **O**　is called a _____.

8) Which hand plays when you see this symbol _____?

LESSON 2

1) Write RH (right hand) or LH (left hand) underneath each staff to show which hand would play for each image.

2) Draw circle note heads on the 5 LINES of the staff

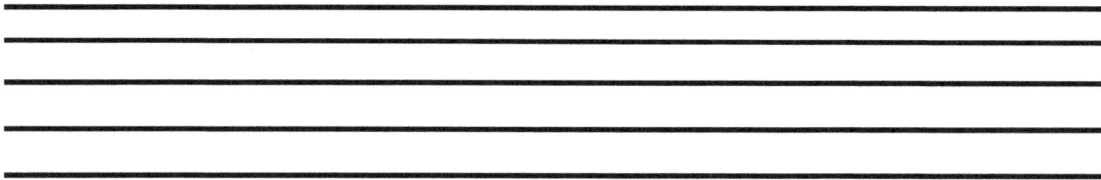

3) Draw The treble clef symbol 3 times

4) Draw the bass clef symbol 3 times

LESSON 3

1) Draw circle note heads on the 4 SPACES of the staff

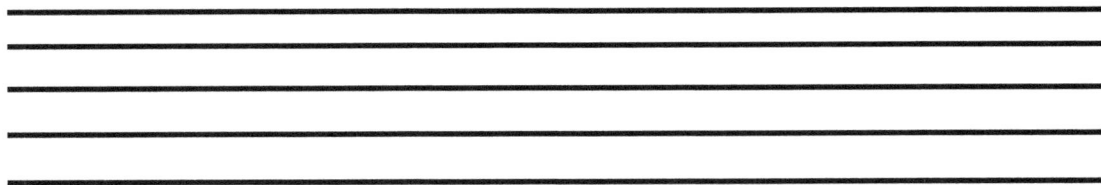

2) Draw a circle around all the bar lines on the music below

3) Bar lines can be on a staff as well. Draw a circle around all the bar lines below

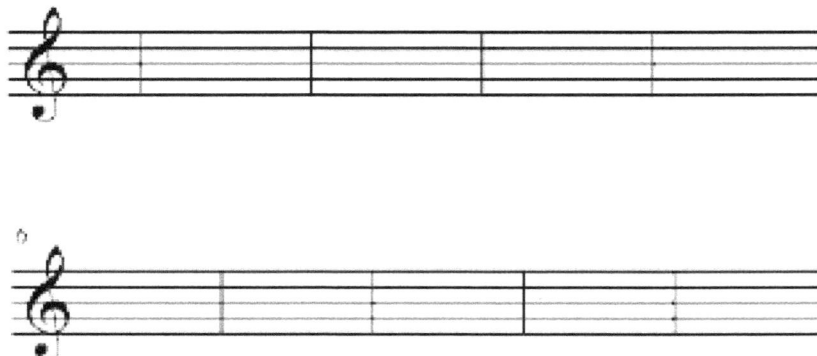

LESSON 4

1) Circle the line notes only

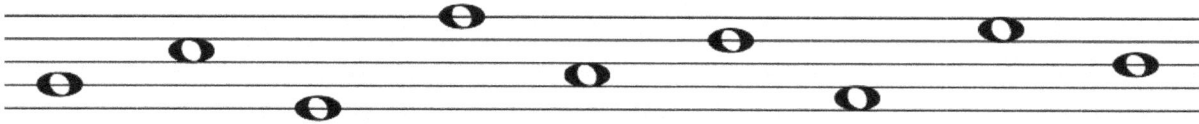

2) How many measures are below _____?

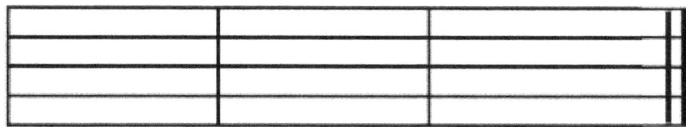

**Final
Double
Bar Line**

3) Circle the space notes only

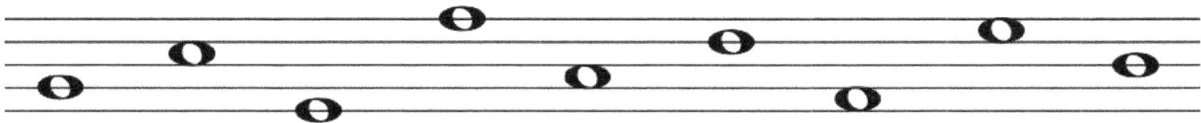

LESSON 5

1) Write **L** below the line notes and **S** below the Space notes

2) Circle the double bar line

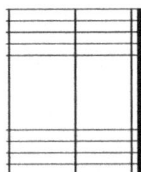

3) How many measures are in the following image _____?

4) Write in the missing counts under each measure (Remember each measure should have a 1 - 2 - 3 - 4

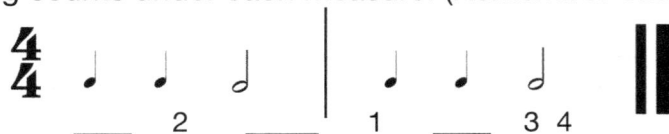

$\frac{4}{4}$ 1 ___ 3 4 | ___ 2 3 4

5) . Write in the missing counts under each measure. (Remember each measure should have a 1 - 2 - 3 - 4)

$\frac{4}{4}$ ___ 2 ___ | 1 ___ 3 4

6) Write in the counts under each measure. (Remember each measure should have a 1 - 2 -3 -4 and some beats get more than one number)

$\frac{4}{4}$

7) Draw in the missing bar lines (Clue: it can help to write in the counts first)

$\frac{4}{4}$

8) Draw a circle note head on either the L (line) or S (space) indicated. Any line/space is fine just don't repeat same note 2x.

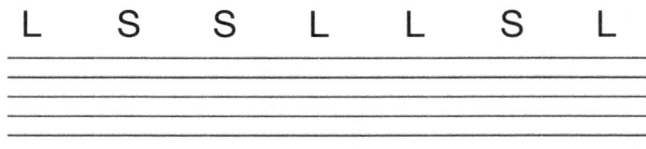

L S S L L S L

LESSON 6

1) How many beats are in a 𝅝 ____?   2) How many beats are in a 𝅗𝅥 _____?

3) How many beats are in a 𝅘𝅥 _____?   4) How many beats are in_____ 𝅗𝅥. ?

5) Matching:

Quarter note   𝅗𝅥.

Half note   𝅘𝅥

Whole note   𝅝   *f*

Forte

Piano   *p*

Dotted half
note   𝅗𝅥

6) Write in the counts under each measure.
(Remember each measure should have a
1 - 2 -3 -4 and some beats get more than one
number)

$\frac{4}{4}$ 𝅘𝅥 𝅘𝅥 𝅗𝅥 | 𝅝 | 𝅗𝅥 𝅗𝅥 ‖

7) Circle the image that has the correct hand
position for C position

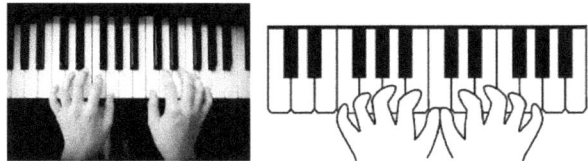

8) Add these note values together.
When added together how many total beats do they receive?   𝅘𝅥 + 𝅗𝅥 =

9) Add these note values together.
When added together how many total beats do they receive?   𝅝 + 𝅗𝅥 =

10) Add these note values together.
When added together how many total beats do they receive?   𝅗𝅥 + 𝅗𝅥 =

11) Add these note values together.
When added together how many total beats do they receive?   𝅝 + 𝅘𝅥 =

CHAPTER 3: Reading music on the treble clef

LESSON 1

1) Write the note you see drawn underneath each note:

2) Draw a note head, 𝗼 , in the proper spot for the letter name designated.

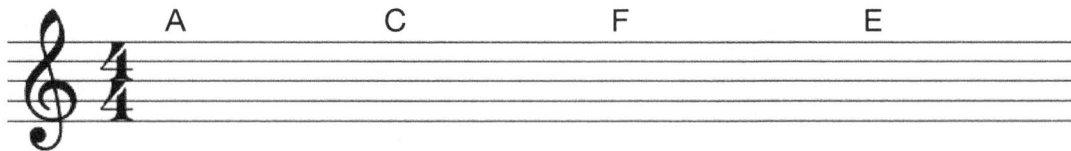

        A   C   F   E

3) Write in the counts under each measure. (Remember each measure should have a 1 - 2 -3 -4 and some beats get more than one number)

LESSON 2

1)   Write the note you see drawn underneath each note:

2)   Just like in your flashcard practice, look at the images below and write the note name underneath them.

3) Draw a note head, 𝄞, in the proper spot for the letter name designated. (Don't forget middle C is in a different location than just plain C).

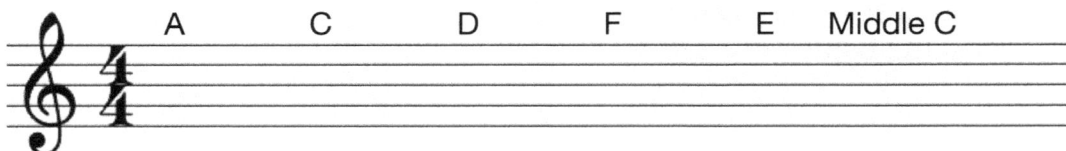

A   C   D   F   E   Middle C

4) Write in the counts under each measure. (Remember each measure should have a 1-2-3-4 and some beats get more than one count)

LESSON 3

1) Just like in your flashcard practice, look at the images below and write the note name underneath them.

2) Write the correct RH finger numbers for the C scale going UP

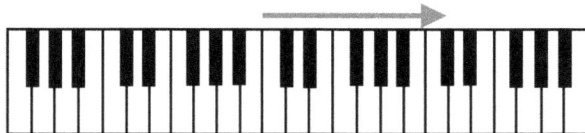

3) Draw a note head, 𝑜 , in the proper spot for the letter name designated. (If you see a letter repeated it means that there are two different locations for that note name… a line note and a space note. Use both your sayings to figure out both locations).

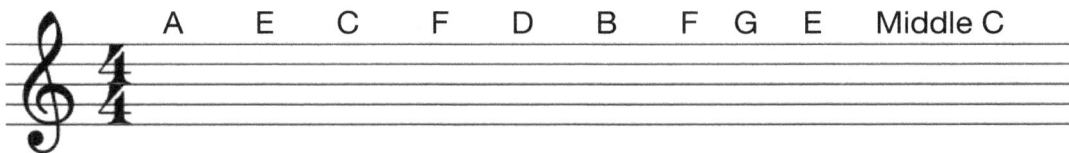

A   E   C   F   D   B   F   G   E   Middle C

LESSON 4

1) Write the correct RH finger numbers for the C scale going DOWN

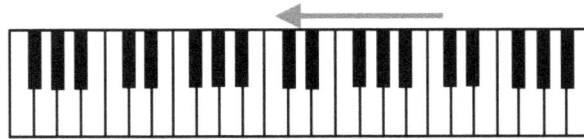

2) Draw a note head, o , in the proper spot for the letter name designated. (If you see a letter repeated it means that there are two different locations for that note name... a line note and a space note. Use both your sayings to figure out both locations).

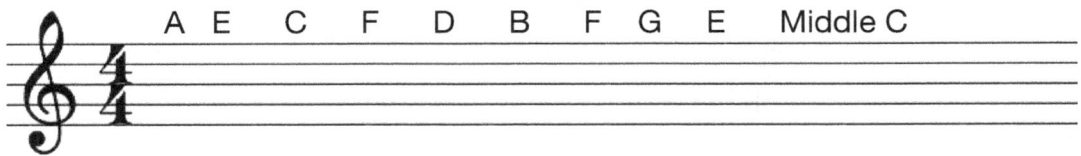

A   E   C   F   D   B   F   G   E   Middle C

3) Just like in your flashcard practice, look at the images below and write the note name underneath them.

4) Write in the counts under each measure. (Remember each measure should have a 1-2-3-4 and some beats get more than one count)

LESSON 5

1) Write the correct RH finger numbers for the C scale going UP

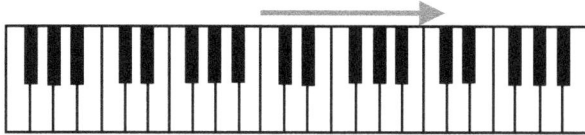

2) Write the correct RH finger numbers for the C scale going DOWN

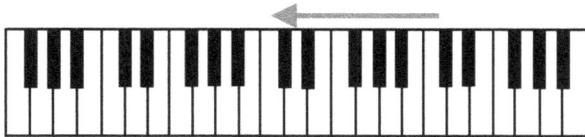

3) Add these note values together. When added how many total beats do they receive?

♩ + 𝅗𝅥 =   𝅗𝅥. + 𝅗𝅥 =

𝅗𝅥. + 𝅝 =   𝅝 + ♩ =

𝅝 + 𝅗𝅥 =   𝅗𝅥 + 𝅗𝅥 =

𝅗𝅥. + ♩ =   𝅗𝅥. + 𝅗𝅥. =

4) Just like in your flashcard practice, look at the images below and write the note name underneath them.

LESSON 6

1) Draw in a bar line every 4 counts to create the missing measures.

2) In each measure, draw a note stepping up the staff.

3) Matching:

Quarter note	♩
Half note	𝅗𝅥.
Whole note	𝅝
Forte	*f*
Piano	*p*
Dotted half note	𝅗𝅥
Mezzo forte	*mf*

4) Write in the counts under each measure. (Remember each measure should have a 1-2-3-4 and some beats get more than one count)

LESSON 7

1)   In each measure, draw a note stepping UP the staff.

2) In each measure, draw a note stepping DOWN the staff.

3) Draw a note head, O , in the proper spot for the letter name designated. (If you see a letter repeated it means that there are two different locations for that note name... a line note and a space note. Use both your sayings to figure out both locations).

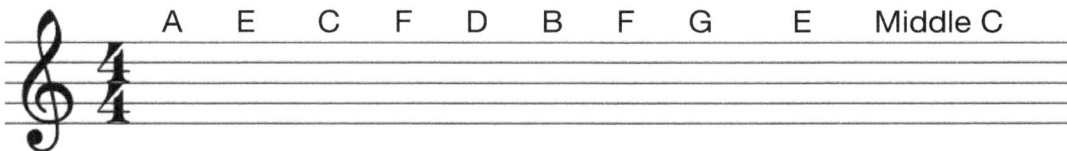

A   E   C   F   D   B   F   G   E   Middle C

4) Draw in a bar line every 4 counts to create the missing measures.

CHAPTER 4: Reading music on the bass clef

LESSON 1

1) Just like in your flashcard practice, look at the images below and write the note name underneath them.

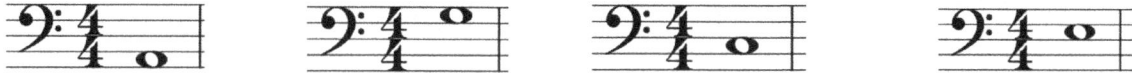

2) In each measure, draw a note stepping UP the staff.

3) In each measure, draw a note stepping DOWN the staff.

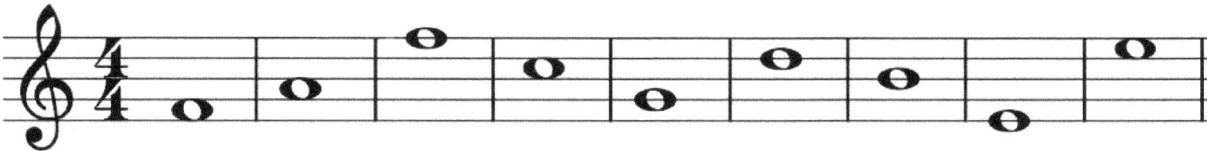

4) Add these note values together. When added how many total beats do they receive?

$$\quarternote + \halfnote =$$

$$\dottedhalf + \halfnote =$$

$$\dottedhalf + \wholenote =$$

$$\wholenote + \quarternote =$$

$$\wholenote + \halfnote =$$

$$\halfnote + \halfnote =$$

$$\dottedhalf + \quarternote =$$

$$\dottedhalf + \dottedhalf =$$

LESSON 2

1) Write the correct LH finger numbers for the C scale going UP

2) Write a **A** over the notes that are played alone and write a **T** above the notes that are played together at the same time.

3) Just like in your flashcard practice, look at the images below and write the note name underneath them.

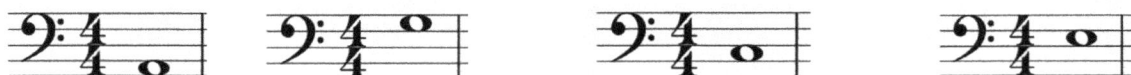

4) Draw a note head, O , in the proper spot for the letter name designated. (If you see a letter repeated it means that there are two different locations for that note name... a line note and a space note. Use both your sayings to figure out both locations).

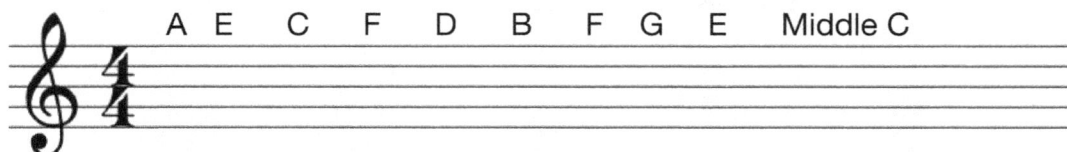

A E   C   F   D   B   F   G   E   Middle C

LESSON 3

1) Just like in your flashcard practice, look at the images below and write the note name underneath them.

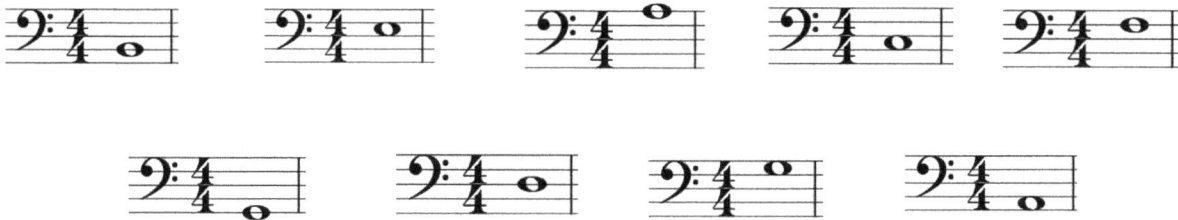

2) Write the correct LH finger numbers for the C scale going UP

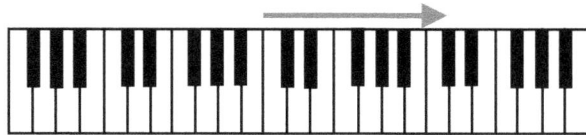

3) In each measure, draw a note stepping DOWN the staff.

4) Write a **A** over the notes that are played alone and write a **T** above the notes that are played together at the same time.

LESSON 4

1) Write the correct LH finger numbers for the C scale going UP

2) Write the correct LH finger numbers for the C scale going Down

3) Just like in your flashcard practice, look at the images below and write the note name underneath them.

4) Write above each measure if the notes are stepping UP, DOWN, or SAME

LESSON 5

1). Write above each measure if the notes are stepping UP, DOWN, or SAME

2) Write above each measure if the notes are played Together or not together.

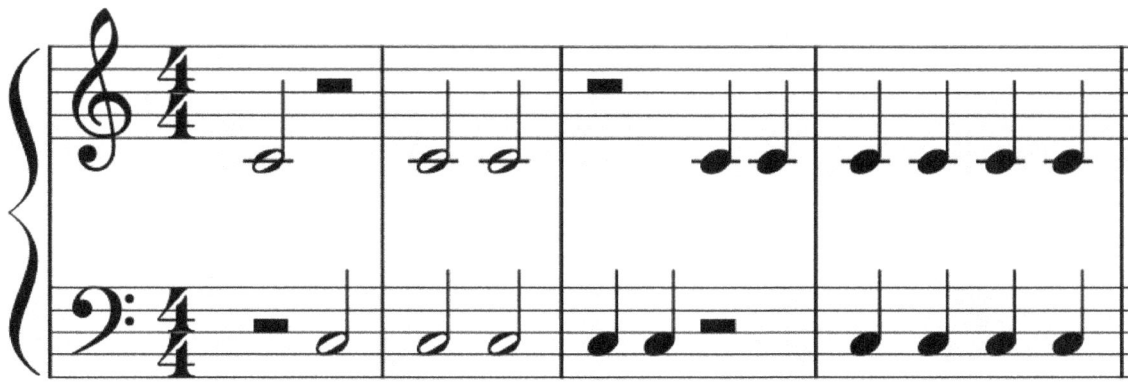

3) Just like in your flashcard practice, look at the images below and write the note name underneath them.

4) Draw in a bar line every 4 counts to create the missing measures.

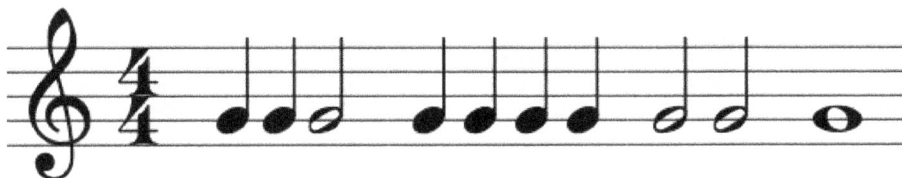

LESSON 6

1) Just like in your flashcard practice, look at the images below and write the note name underneath them.

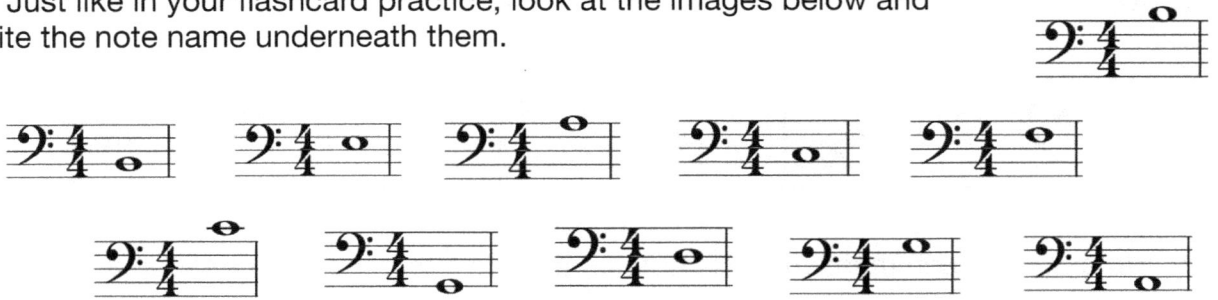

2) Draw a note head, 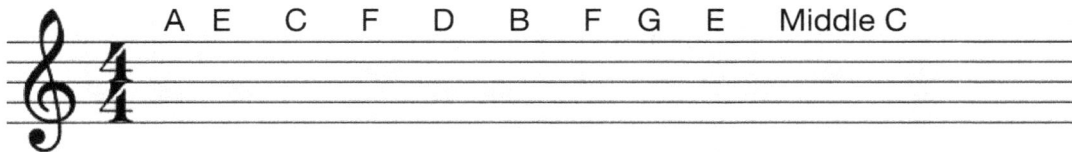 , in the proper spot for the letter name designated. (If you see a letter repeated it means that there are two different locations for that note name… a line note and a space note. Use both your sayings to figure out both locations).

A E   C   F   D   B   F   G   E   Middle C

3) Matching:

Repeat

Quarter note

Half note

Whole note

Slur

Forte

Piano

Dotted half note

Mezzo forte

Grand staff

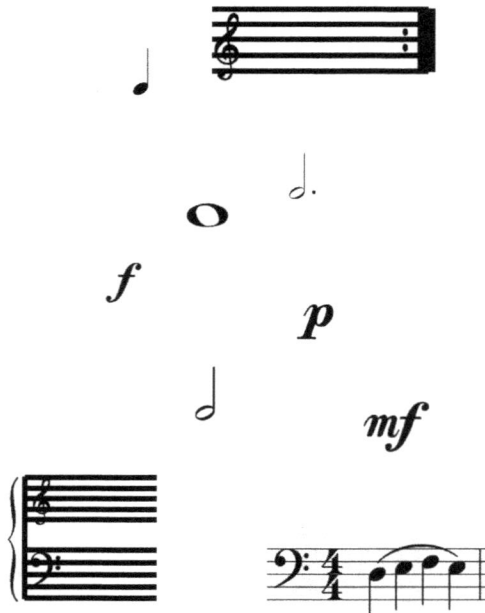

CHAPTER 5: Skips verses steps in music

LESSON 1

1)   Write in the counts under each measure. (Remember each measure should have a 1 - 2 -3 and some beats get more than one number)

2)   Circle all examples that show a step on the piano.

3)   Circle all examples that show a skip on the piano

4)   Write if the notes are stepping up (U), down (D) , or staying the same (S) in each measure

5)   Write in the counts to this song (this song is this weeks practice song so let this be a theory be a guide in your practice)

6)   Draw a note head, ○ in the proper spot for the letter name designated. (If you see a letter repeated it means that there are two different locations for that note name… a line note and a space note. Use both your sayings to figure out both locations).

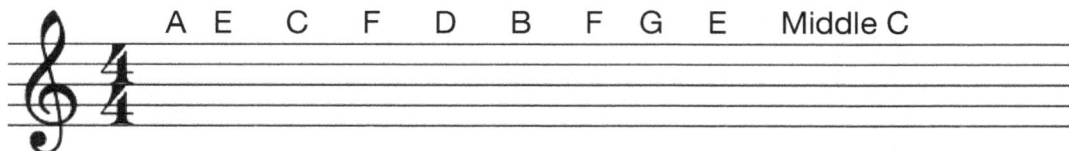

A E   C   F   D   B   F   G   E   Middle C

7) Draw in a bar line every 3 counts to create the missing measures.

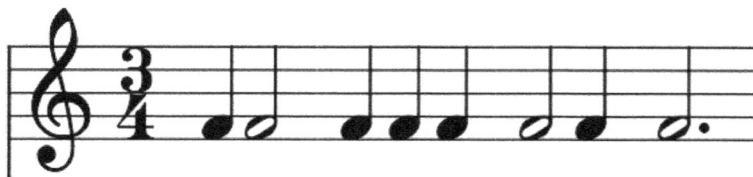

LESSON 2

1) Write in the counts under each measure. (Watch the time signature)

2) Write in the counts under each measure. (Watch the time signature)

3) Write in the counts to this song (this song is this weeks practice song so let this be a theory be a guide in your practice)

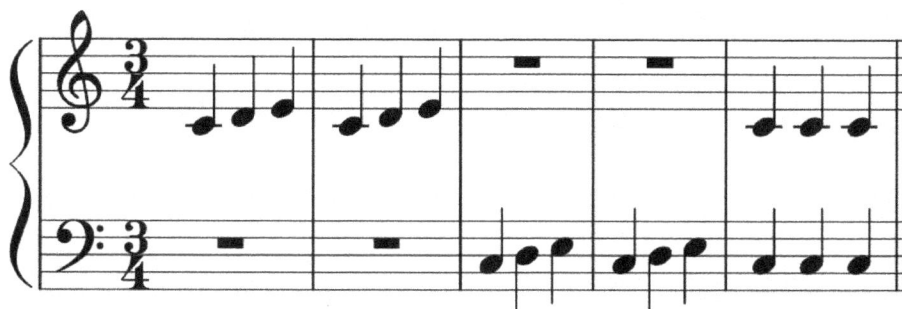

4) Draw a note head, o , in the proper spot for the letter name designated. (If you see a letter repeated it means that there are two different locations for that note name... a line note and a space note. Use both your sayings to figure out both locations).

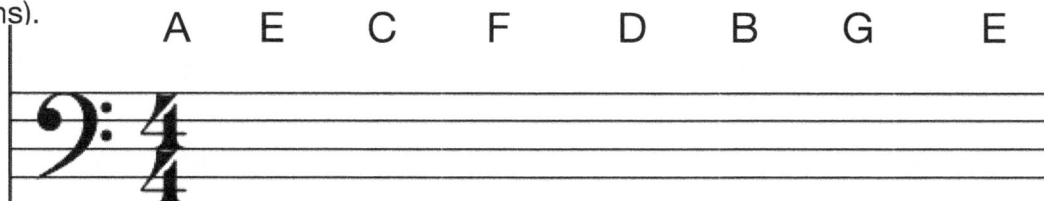

A   E   C   F   D   B   G   E

5) In each measure, draw a note stepping UP the staff.

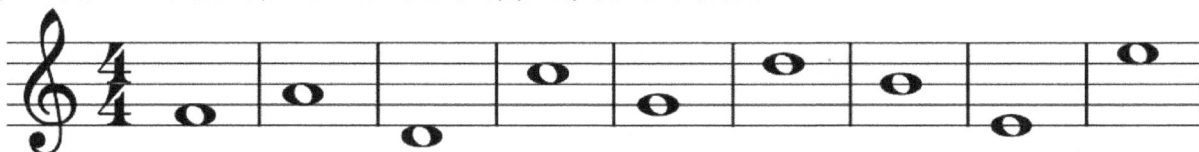

6) In each measure, draw a note stepping DOWN the staff.

LESSON 3

1) Write if the notes are stepping, skipping or staying the same.

2) Draw a note skipping UP in each measure from the note that is drawn

3) Draw a note skipping DOWN in each measure from the note that is drawn

4) Write in the counts to this song (this song is this weeks practice song so let this be a theory be a guide in your practice)

5) Matching:

Quarter
Repeat
Half note
Whole note
Slur
Forte
Piano
Dotted half note
Grand staff
Mezzo Forte

LESSON 4

1) Write step or skip in between each note.

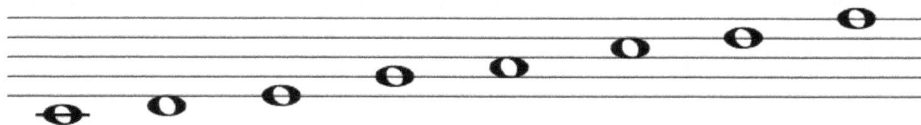

2) Write step or skip under each measure.
3) Write step or skip in between each note

4) Write in the counts to this song (this song is this weeks practice song so let this be a theory be a guide in your practice)

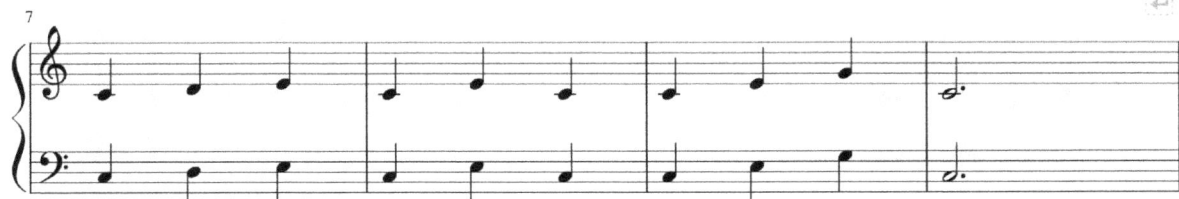

LESSON 5

1) Write step or skip underneath each measure.

2) Circle all examples below that show a step on the piano.

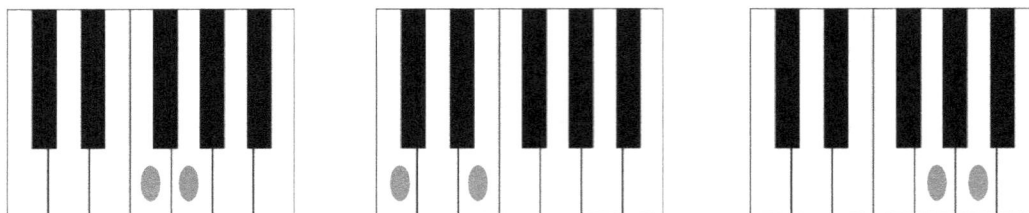

3)   Circle all examples below that show a skip on the piano

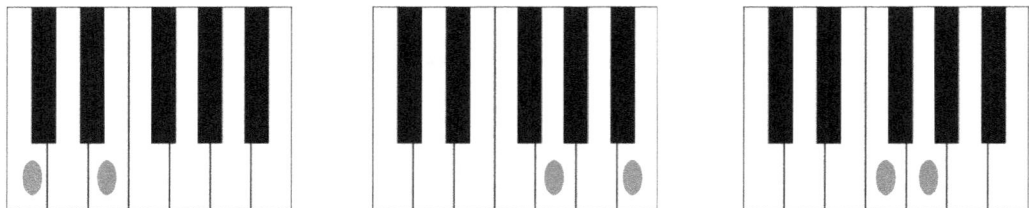

4) Write in the counts to this song (this song is this weeks practice song so let this be a theory be a guide in your practice)

LESSON 6

1) In each measure, draw a note stepping UP the staff.

2) In each measure, draw a note stepping DOWN the staff.

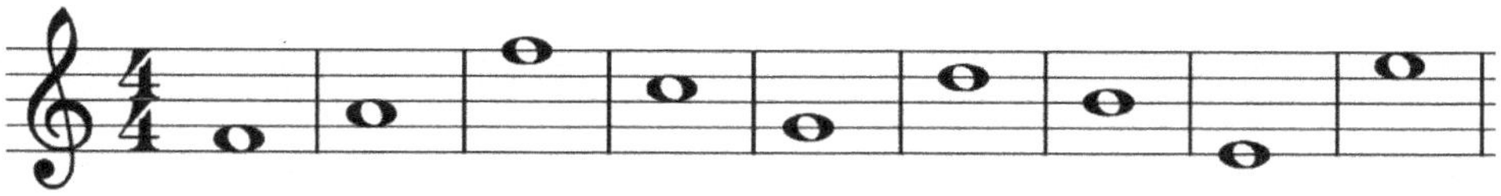

3) Just like in your flashcard practice, look at the images below and write the note name underneath them.

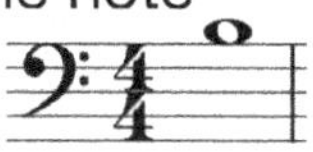

4) Add these note values together. When added how many total beats do they receive?

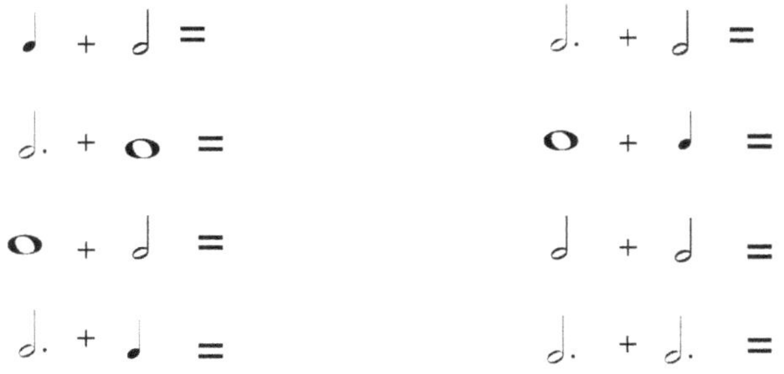

4) Write in the counts to this song (this song is this weeks practice song so let this be a theory be a guide in your practice)

CHAPTER 6: Finding on the piano the notes on the staff

LESSON 1

1) Write in the counts and the missing bar line for the rhythm below

$\dfrac{3}{4}$ 𝅗𝅥. 𝅘𝅥 𝅘𝅥 𝅘𝅥 𝅗𝅥 𝅘𝅥 𝅘𝅥 𝅘𝅥 𝅗𝅥. ‖

2) write in the number for how many beats you would hold the tied note for:

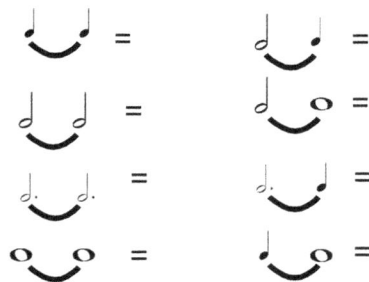

𝅘𝅥 ⌣ 𝅘𝅥 =   𝅗𝅥 ⌣ 𝅘𝅥. =

𝅗𝅥 ⌣ 𝅗𝅥 =   𝅗𝅥 ⌣ 𝅝 =

𝅗𝅥. ⌣ 𝅗𝅥. =   𝅗𝅥. ⌣ 𝅘𝅥 =

𝅝 ⌣ 𝅝 =   𝅘𝅥 ⌣ 𝅝 =

3) Write in the counts for the rhythm below. Then draw a star under where the claps will go when counting aloud. Then clap and count it aloud.

$\dfrac{4}{4}$ 𝅘𝅥 𝅘𝅥 𝅘𝅥 𝅘𝅥 ⌣ 𝅘𝅥 𝅗𝅥 𝅗𝅥 ⌣ 𝅘𝅥 𝅘𝅥 𝅘𝅥 ⌣ 𝅝 ‖

4). Write in the counts to this song (this song is this weeks practice song so let this be a theory be a guide in your practice)

5) Just like in your flashcard practice, look at the images below and write the note name underneath them.

LESSON 2

1) Write in the counts for the rhythm below. Then draw a star under where the claps will go when counting aloud. Then clap and count it aloud.

2) Write if the notes are located in the bass, middle or treble section of the piano

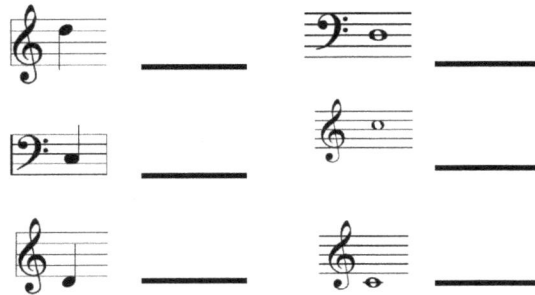

3) Write in the counts to this song (this song is this weeks practice song so let this be a theory be a guide in your practice)

4) In each measure, draw a note stepping UP the staff.

5) In each measure, draw a note stepping DOWN the staff.

LESSON 3

1) Write S for slur and T for Tie above each curved line to identify which are slurs and which are ties.

2) Write in the counts to this song (this song is this weeks practice song so let this be a theory be a guide in your practice)

3) Write S below the curved lines that are Slurs and T below the curved lines that are ties.

UP   DOWN

4) Draw a star on the note where the tunnel happens and 3rd finger hopping over happens in both hands going up and going down. Make sure to play it on your piano after you have written it down

RIGHT HAND

UP   DOWN

LEFT HAND
 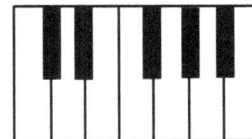

LESSON 4

1). Write S below
the curved lines
that are Slurs and T
below the curved
lines that are ties.

2) Write under each
note if the note is
located in the bass (B),
middle (M) or treble (T)
section of the piano.

3). Write S below the curved lines that are Slurs and T below the curved lines that are
ties.

4)Write in the counts to this song (this song is this weeks practice song so let this be a
theory be a guide in your practice)

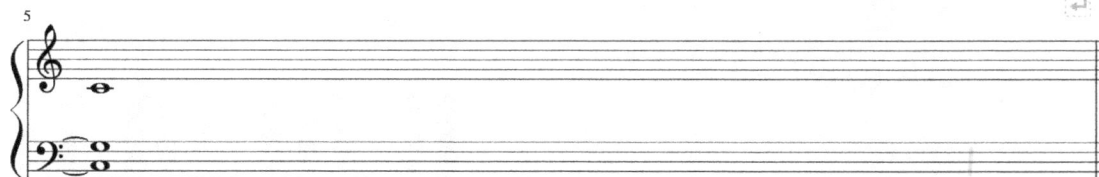

CHAPTER 7: The quarter rest

Lesson 1

1) Write under each note if the note is located in the bass (B), middle (M) or treble (T) section of the piano.

2) Just like in your flashcard practice, look at the images below and write the note name underneath them.

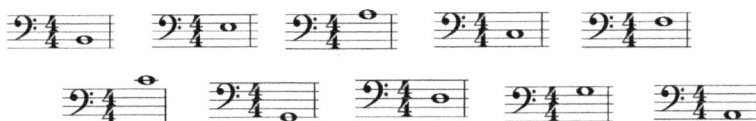

3) Draw circle note heads starting from middle C and going up 1 additional STEPS (C-D)

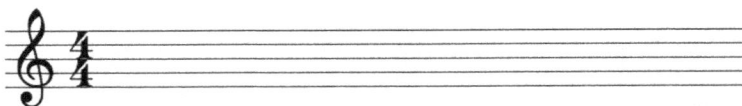

4) write in the number for how many beats you would hold the tied note for

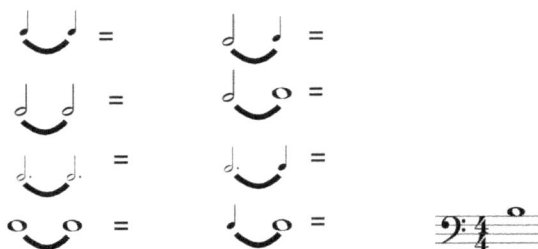

5). Just like in your flashcard practice, look at the images below and write the note name underneath them.

6)Write in the counts to this song (this song is this weeks practice song so let this be a theory be a guide in your practice)

Lesson 2

1) is the example below 3/4 time or 4/4 time? _____

2) is the example below 3/4 time or 4/4 time? _____

3)is the example below 3/4 time or 4/4 time? _____

4)is the example below 3/4 time or 4/4 time?_____

5) write in counts underneath.

6) Draw circle note heads starting from middle C and going up 3 additional STEPS (C-D-E)

7) Write in the counts to this song (this song is this weeks practice song so let this be a theory be a guide in your practice)

LESSON 3

1) Write in the counts under
   neath the rhythm below.
   Then add a star under each
   spot that receives a clap.
   Then clap and count this rhythm aloud.

2) Draw in the notes below. note: All C's refer to bass c and not middle C

C   G   D   B   E   A   F

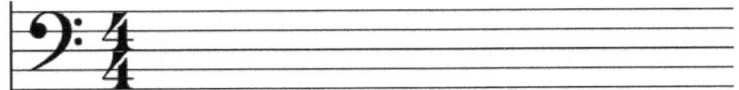

3) Draw in the notes below. note: All C's refer to treble c and not middle C

C   G   D   B   E   A   F

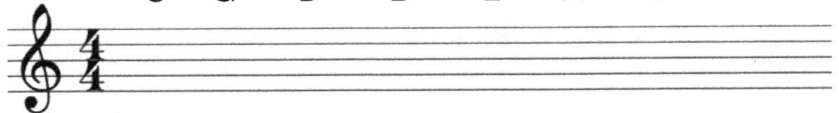

4) Write in the counts under neath the rhythm below. Then add a star under each spot
that receives a clap. Then clap and count this rhythm aloud. Then   play the
rhythm on a middle C note
with the right hand 1 finger.

5) Write in the counts
to this song (this song
is this weeks practice
song so let this be a
theory be a guide in
your practice)

6) Draw circle note
heads starting from middle C and going up 4 additional STEPS (C-D-E-F)

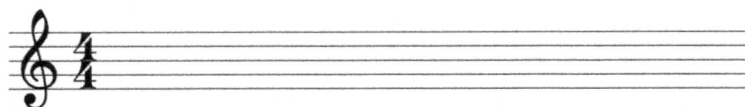

LESSON 4

1) Write in the counts under neath the rhythm below. Then add a star under each spot that receives a clap. Then clap and count this rhythm aloud. Then play the rhythm on the correct notes

2) Draw circle note heads starting from middle C and going up 5 additional STEPS (C-D-E-F-G)

3) Write in the counts to this song (this song is this weeks practice song so let this be a theory be a guide in your practice)

LESSON 5

1) Draw circle note heads starting from middle C and going up 6 additional STEPS (C-D-E-F-G -A)

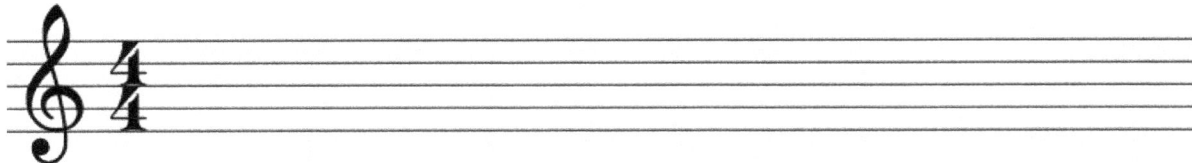

2) Draw a quarter note _____

3) Draw a half note _____

4) Draw a whole note _____

5) Draw a quarter rest _____

6) Draw a dotted half note _____

7) Write in the counts to this song (this song is this weeks practice song so let this be a theory be a guide in your practice)

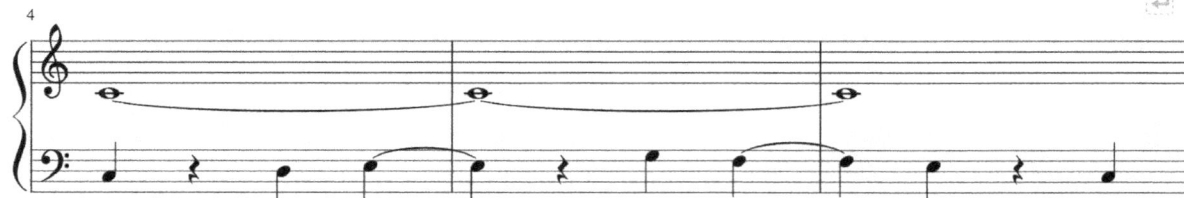

CHAPTER 8: Staccatos and Accidentals

LESSON 1

1) Draw the note that gets 1 beat _____

2). Draw the note that gets 4 beats _____

3) Draw the note that gets 3 beats _____

4) Draw the note that gets 2 beats _____

5) Draw the rest that gets 1 beat _____

6) Draw circle note heads starting from middle C and going up 7 additional STEPS (C-D-E-F-G -A - B)

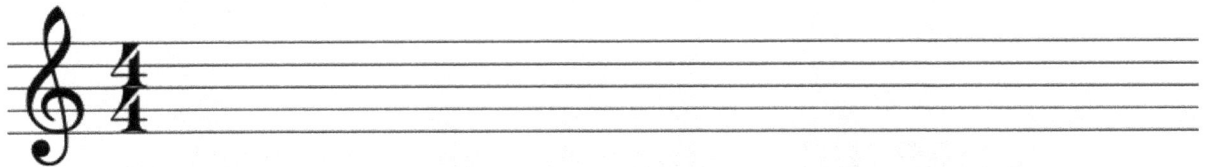

7) Write in the counts under neath the rhythm below. Then add a star under each spot that receives a clap. Then clap and count this rhythm aloud. Then play the rhythm on the correct notes

8) Write in the counts to this song (this song is this weeks practice song so let this be a theory be a guide in your practice)

9) Write in the name of the note below each note that is drawn.

LESSON 2

1) Draw circle note heads starting from middle C and going up 8 additional STEPS (C-D-E-F-G -A - B - C) You have just drawn the C scale going up

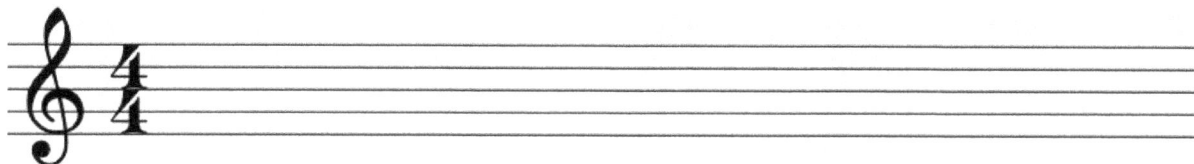

2) Now that you can draw your C scale going up, you can draw it going down as well. On the staff below, start at treble C (the note you ended on on problem #1 above). Then step down 8 steps until you reach middle C. This is drawing the C scale going down.

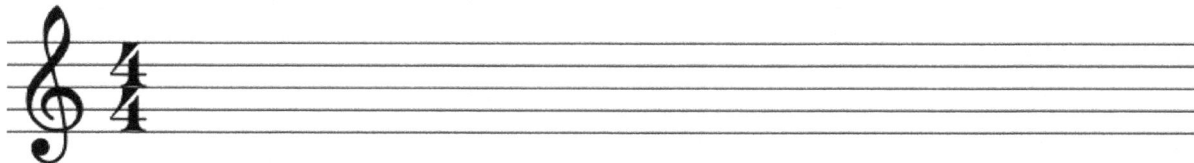

3) Write in the name of the note below each note drawn.

4) Write in the name of the note below each note that is drawn.

5) Circle a C#

6) Circle a B♭

7) Circle a F#

8) Circle a D♭

9) Write in the counts to this song (this song is this weeks practice song so let this be a theory be a guide in your practice)

LESSON 3

1) Circle a D #

2) Circle a E♭

3) Circle a G#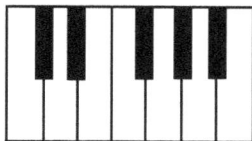

4) Circle a A♭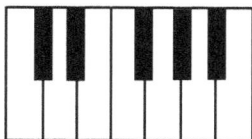

5) Draw a C Scale going up on the first staff and a C scale going down on the second staff.

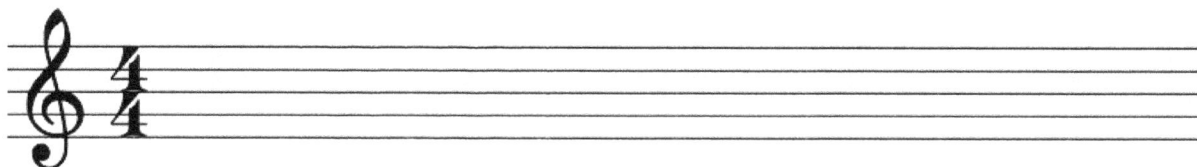

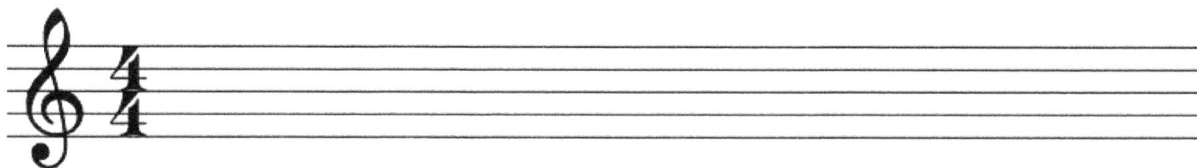

6) Write in the counts to this song (this song is this weeks practice song so let this be a theory be a guide in your practice)

LESSON 4

1) Matching:

2) Write in the counts to this song (this song is this weeks practice song so let this be a theory be a guide in your practice)

3) Draw a C scale going up then down on the same staff

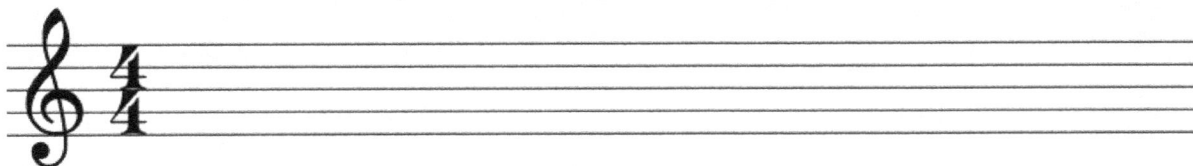

4) Write in the name of the note below each note drawn.

5) Write in the name of the note below each note that is drawn.

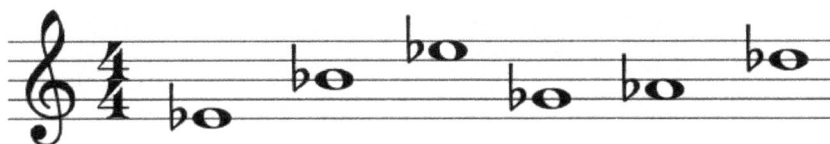

6) Draw the note that gets 1 beat _____   11) Draw a quarter note _____

7). Draw the note that gets 4 beats _____   12) Draw a half note _____

8) Draw the note that gets 3 beats _____   13) Draw a whole note _____

9) Draw the note that gets 2 beats _____   14) Draw a quarter rest _____

10) Draw the rest that gets 1 beat _____   15) Draw a dotted half note _____

16) Draw in the notes below. note: All C's refer to bass c and not middle C

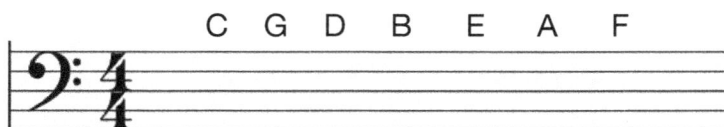

                                    C G D B E A F

17) Draw in the notes below. note: All C's refer to treble c and not middle C

                                C G D B E A F

ANSWER KEY

CHAPTER 1: Learning the Basics

LESSON 1 (Answers)

1. Color the Right hand BLUE and color the left hand RED

2. Write in the correct finger numbers above each finger in the left and right hand

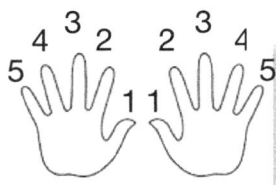

3. Color the low end of the piano BLUE and the high end of the piano RED

    BLUE   RED

4. Circle all the groups of 2 black notes

5. Circle all the groups of 3 black notes

LESSON 2 (Answers)

1. Which finger number is the arrow pointing to on each RIGHT hand image.

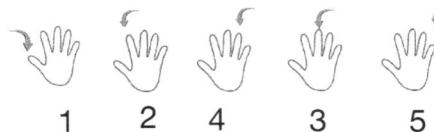

    1   2   4   3   5

2. Which finger number is the arrow point to on each LEFT hand image

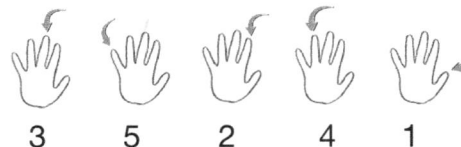

    3   5   2   4   1

3) Circle all the groups of 2 black notes

4) Color all The C's on the piano

5) Matching:

    QUARTER

    HALF NOTE

    WHOLE NOTE

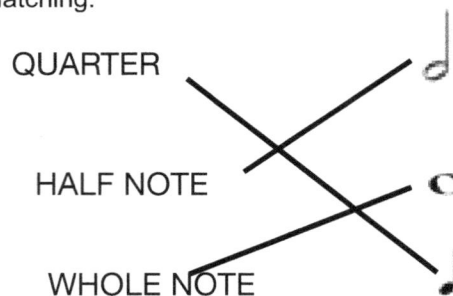

6) How many beats in a ♩ __1____?

7) How many beats in a o ____4__ ?

8) How many beats in a ♩ ___2____?

LESSON 3

1) Color all the C's on the piano

2) Color all the D's on the piano

3) Color all the E's on the piano

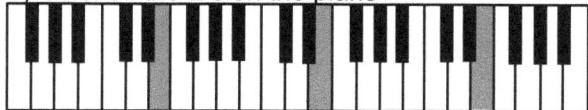

4) Color all the F's on the piano

5) Color all the G's on the piano

6) Color all the A's on the piano

7) Color all the B's on the piano

LESSON 4

1) Are the notes going up or going down?

__UP_____

2) Are the notes going up or going down?

___DOWN_____

3) _p_ stands for the word __PIANO____ and means to play __SOFTLY_____.

4) _f_ stands for the word __FORTE____ and means to play ___LOUDLY____.

5) Color the D's red, the F's blue and the A's yellow.

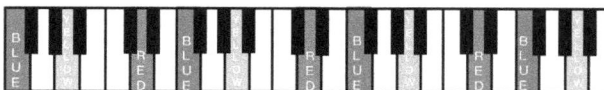

6) Color the E's red, the G's blue and the B's yellow.

LESSON 5

1) Color the D's red, the F's blue and the A's yellow.

2) Color the E's red, the G's blue and the B's yellow.

3) Are the notes going up, down, or staying the same? __DOWN_____

4) Are the notes going up, down, or staying the same? ___SAME_____

5) Are the notes going up, down, or staying the same? ____UP____

LESSON 6

1) Color the D's red, the F's blue and the A's yellow.

2) Color the E's red, the G's blue and the B's yellow.

3) Matching

Quarter note
Piano
Whole note
Forte
Half note

𝆹 𝆑 𝆺 𝅝 𝒑

CHAPTER 2: Lines, Spaces and Counting Music

LESSON 1

1) 𝄞 is called _____TREBLE CLEF__.

2) ☰ is called a STAFF_____.

3) 𝒇 is called _____FORTE_____.

4) 𝒑 is called _____PIANO_____.

5). 𝅗𝅥 is called a ____HALF NOTE__.

6) ♩ is called a ___QUARTER NOTE___.

7). 𝅝 is called a ____WHOLE NOTE_____

8) Which hand plays when you see this symbol

_____RIGHT_____ 𝄞

LESSON 2

1) Write RH (right hand) or LH (left hand) underneath each staff to show which hand would play for each image.

𝄞 𝄢 𝄞 𝄢 𝄢

RH   LH   RH   LH   LH

2) Draw circle note heads on the 5 LINES of the staff

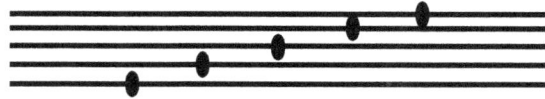

3) Draw The treble clef symbol 3 times

𝄞   𝄞   𝄞

4) Draw the bass clef symbol 3 times

𝄢 𝄢 𝄢

LESSON 3

1) Draw circle note heads on the 4 SPACES of the staff

2) Draw a circle around all the bar lines on the music below

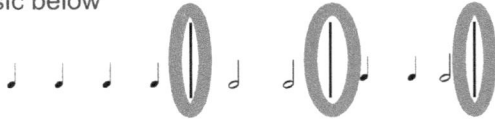

3) Bar lines can be on a staff as well. Draw a circle around all the bar lines below

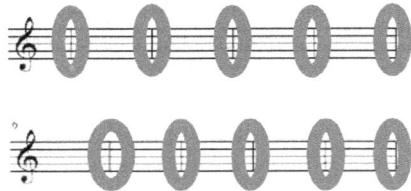

LESSON 4

1) Circle the line notes only

2) How many measures are below

_____3_____?

Final
Double
Bar Line

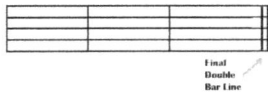

3) Circle the space notes only

LESSON 5

1) Write **L** below the line notes and **S** below the Space notes

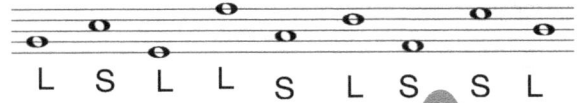

L   S   L   L   S   L   S   S   L

2) Circle the double bar line

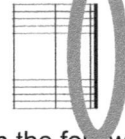

3) How many measures are in the following image

_____2_____?

4) Write in the missing counts under each measure (Remember each measure should have a 1 - 2 - 3 - 4)

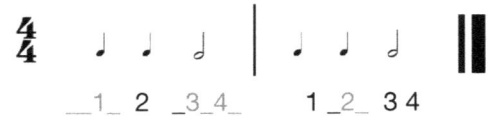

4/4

1   2 . 3 4 _1_   2   3   4

5) . Write in the missing counts under each measure. (Remember each measure should have a 1 -2 -3 -4)

4/4

__1_ 2 _3_4_   1 _2_ 3 4

6) Write in the counts under each measure. (Remember each measure should have a 1 - 2 -3 -4 and some beats get more than one number)

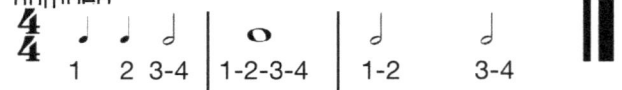

4/4

1   2 3-4 | 1-2-3-4 | 1-2   3-4

7) Draw in the missing bar lines (Clue: it can help to write in the counts first)

4/4

8) Draw a circle note head on either the L (line) or S (space) indicated. Any line/space is fine just don't repeat same note 2x. (ANSWERS WILL VARY)

L   S   S   L   L   S L

LESSON 6

1) How many beats are in a 𝅝 _____4_____ ?

2) How many beats are in a 𝅗𝅥 _____2_____ ?

3) How many beats are in a ♩ _____1_____ ?

4) How many beats are in a 𝅗𝅥. ____3_____ ?'

5) Matching:

Quarter note
Half note
Whole note
Forte
Piano
Dotted half note

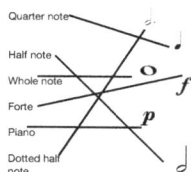

6) Write in the counts under each measure. (Remember each measure should have a 1 - 2 -3 -4 and some beats get more than one number)

$\frac{4}{4}$ ♩ ♩ 𝅗𝅥 | 𝅝 | 𝅗𝅥 𝅗𝅥 ‖

1 2 3-4. 1-2-3-4 1-2 3-4

7) Circle the image that has the correct hand position for C position

8) Add these note values together. When added together how many total beats do they receive?

♩ + 𝅗𝅥 = 3

9) Add these note values together. When added together how many total beats do they receive?

𝅝 + 𝅗𝅥 = 6

10) Add these note values together. When added together how many total beats do they receive?

𝅗𝅥 + 𝅗𝅥 = 4

11) Add these note values together. When added together how many total beats do they receive?

𝅝 + ♩ = 5

Chapter 3: READING MUSIC ON THE TREBLE CLEF

LESSON 1

1) Write the note you see drawn underneath each note:

F   A   C   E

2) Draw a note head, 𝅝 , in the proper spot for the letter name designated.

A   C   F   E

3) Write in the counts under each measure. (Remember each measure should have a 1 - 2 -3 -4 and some beats get more than one number)

$\frac{4}{4}$ ♩ ♩ 𝅗𝅥 | 𝅝 | ♩ 𝅗𝅥. ‖

1 2. 3-4 1-2-3-4 1 2-3-4

LESSON 2

1) Write the note you see drawn underneath each note:

F　C　E　A　D　C

2) Just like in your flashcard practice, look at the images below and write the note name underneath them.

D　　C　　E

A　　F　　C

3) Draw a note head, ○ , in the proper spot for the letter name designated. (Don't forget middle C is in a different location than just plain C).

A　C　D　F　E　MIDDLE C

4) Write in the counts under each measure. (Remember each measure should have a 1-2-3-4 and some beats get more than one count)

1 2 3-4 1-2 3 4　1-2　3-4　1-2-3-4

LESSON 3

1) Just like in your flashcard practice, look at the images below and write the note name underneath them.

E　F　D　C　G　C

D　B　A　F　E

2) Write the correct RH finger numbers for the C scale going UP

1 2 3 1 2 3 4 5

3) Draw a note head, , in the proper spot for the letter name designated. (If you see a letter repeated it means that there are two different locations for that note name... a line note and a space note. Use both your sayings to figure out both locations). ANSWERS WILL VARY

A E C F D B F G E MIDDLE C

Stephanie Parker

LESSON 4

1) Write the correct RH finger numbers for the C scale going DOWN

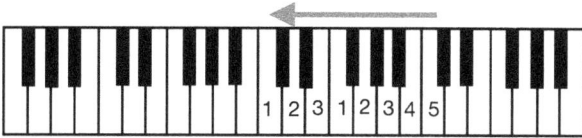

1 2 3 1 2 3 4 5

2) Draw a note head, o , in the proper spot for the letter name designated. (If you see a letter repeated it means that there are two different locations for that note name... a line note and a space note. Use both your sayings to figure out both locations). ANSWERS WILL VARY

A E C F D B F G E MIDDLE C

3) Just like in your flashcard practice, look at the images below and write the note name underneath them.

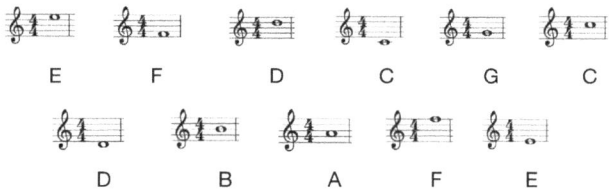

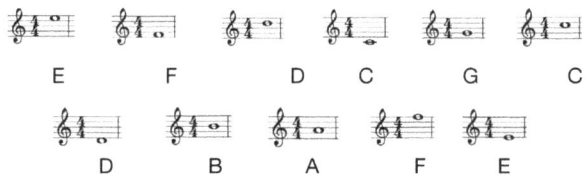

E   F   D   C   G   C

D   B   A   F   E

4) Write in the counts under each measure. (Remember each measure should have a 1-2-3-4 and some beats get more than one count)

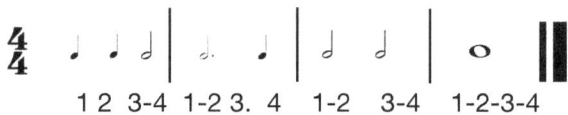

4/4

1 2 3-4 1-2 3. 4 1-2 3-4 1-2-3-4

LESSON 5

1) Write the correct RH finger numbers for the C scale going UP

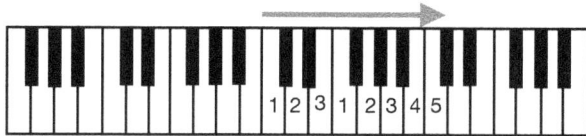

1 2 3 1 2 3 4 5

2) Write the correct RH finger numbers for the C scale going DOWN

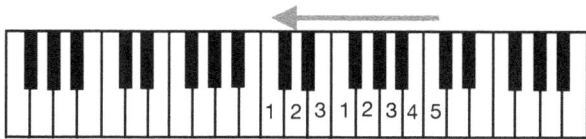

1 2 3 1 2 3 4 5

3) Add these note values together. When added how many total beats do they receive?

♩ + ♩ = 3   ♩. + ♩ = 5

♩. + o = 7   o + ♩ = 5

o + ♩ = 6   ♩ + ♩ = 4

♩. + ♩ = 4   ♩. + ♩. = 6

4) Just like in your flashcard practice, look at the images below and write the note name underneath them.

E   F   D   C   G   C

D   B   A   F   E

64

LESSON 6

1) Draw in a bar line every 4 counts to create the missing measures.

2) In each measure, draw a note stepping up the staff.

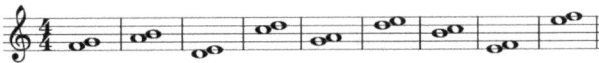

3) matching

Quarter note

Half note

Whole note

Forte

Piano

Dotted half
note

Mezzo forte

LESSON 7

1) In each measure, draw a note stepping UP the staff.

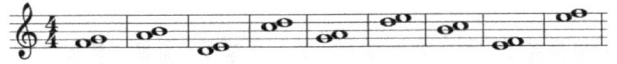

2) In each measure, draw a note stepping DOWN the staff.

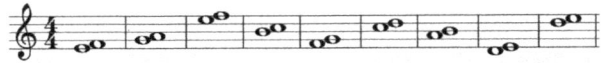

3) Draw a note head, o , in the proper spot for the letter name designated. (If you see a letter repeated it means that there are two different locations for that note name… a line note and a space note. Use both your sayings to figure out both locations).

A E C   F D B F G   E MIDDLE C

4) Draw in a bar line every 4 counts to create the missing measures.

4) Write in the counts under each measure. (Remember each measure should have a 1-2-3-4 and some beats get more than one count)

1   2-3-4   1 2 3 -4 1-2 3-4   1-2-3-4

Chapter 4: READING MUSIC ON THE BASS CLEF

LESSON 1

1) Just like in your flashcard practice, look at the images below and write the note name underneath them.

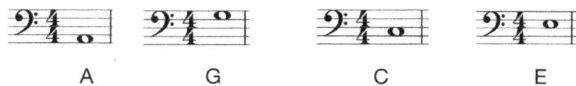

A G C E

2) In each measure, draw a note stepping UP the staff.

3) In each measure, draw a note stepping DOWN the staff.

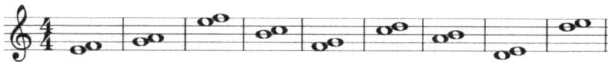

4) Add these note values together. When added how many total beats do they receive?

♩ + 𝅗𝅥 = 3   𝅗𝅥. + 𝅗𝅥 = 5

𝅗𝅥. + 𝅝 = 7   𝅝 + ♩ = 5

𝅝 + 𝅗𝅥 = 6   𝅗𝅥 + 𝅗𝅥 = 4

𝅗𝅥. + ♩ = 4   𝅗𝅥. + 𝅗𝅥. = 6

LESSON 2

1) Write the correct LH finger numbers for the C scale going UP

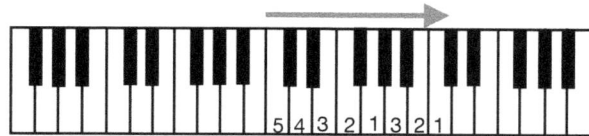

5 4 3 2 1 3 2 1

2) Write a **A** over the notes that are played alone and write a **T** above the notes that are played together at the same time

A A T A A T

3) Just like in your flashcard practice, look at the images below and write the note name underneath them.

A G C E

4) Draw a note head, 𝅗𝅥 , in the proper spot for the letter name designated. (If you see a letter repeated it means that there are two different locations for that note name... a line note and a space note. Use both your sayings to figure out both locations).

A E C F D B F G E MIDDLE C

LESSON 3

1) Just like in your flashcard practice, look at the images below and write the note name underneath them.

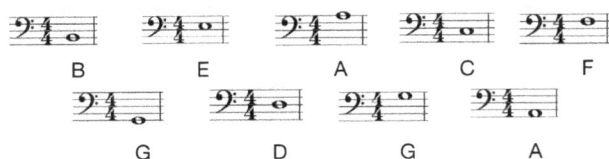

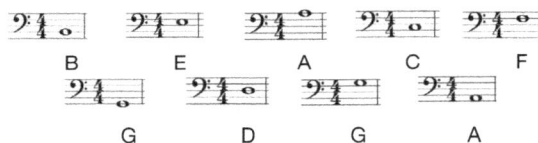

B   E   A   C   F

G   D   G   A

2) Write the correct LH finger numbers for the C scale going UP

5 4 3 2 1 3 2 1

3) In each measure, draw a note stepping DOWN the staff.

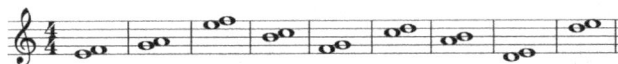

4) Write a **A** over the notes that are played alone and write a **T** above the notes that are played together at the same time.

A A T   A A T

LESSON 4

1) Write the correct LH finger numbers for the C scale going UP

5 4 3 2 1 3 2 1

2) Write the correct LH finger numbers for the C scale going Down

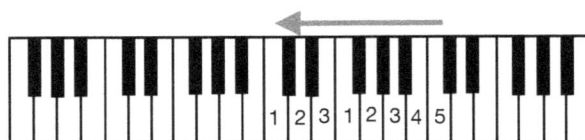

1 2 3 1 2 3 4 5

3) Just like in your flashcard practice, look at the images below and write the note name underneath them.

B   E   A   C   F

G   D   G   A

4) Write above each measure if the notes are stepping UP, DOWN, or SAME

SAME   UP   DOWN

LESSON 5

1). Write above each measure if the notes are stepping UP, DOWN, or SAME

SAME   UP   DOWN   UP   SAME   DOWN

2) Write above each measure if the notes are played Together or not together.

NOT Together   Together   NOT Together   Together

3) Just like in your flashcard practice, look at the images below and write the note name underneath them.

B   E   A   C   F

C   G   D   G   A

B

4) Draw in a bar line every 4 counts to create the missing measures.

LESSON 6

1) Just like in your flashcard practice, look at the images below and write the note name underneath them.

B   E   A   C   F

C   G   D   G   A

B

2) Draw a note head, ○ , in the proper spot for the letter name designated. (If you see a letter repeated it means that there are two different locations for that note name… a line note and a space note. Use both your sayings to figure out both locations).

A   E   C   F   D   B   F   G   E   MIDDLE C

3) Matching:

Repeat

Quarter note

Half note

Whole note

Slur

Forte

Piano

Dotted half note

Mezzo Forte

Grand staff

Chapter 5: SKIPS VERSES STEPS IN MUSIC

LESSON 1

1) Write in the counts under each measure. (Remember each measure should have a 1 - 2 -3 and some beats get more than one number)

2) Circle all examples below that show a step on the piano.

3) Circle all examples below that show a skip on the piano

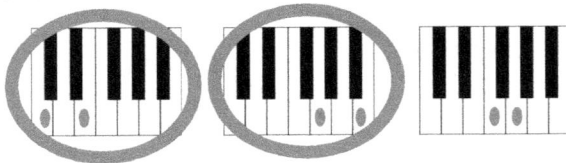

4) Write if the notes are stepping up (U), down (D), or staying the same (S) in each measure

5) Write in the counts to this song (this song is this weeks practice song so let this be a theory be a guide in your practice)

5) Draw a note head, ○ , in the proper spot for the letter name designated. (If you see a letter repeated it means that there are two different locations for that note name… a line note and a space note. Use both your sayings to figure out both locations).

6) Draw in a bar line every 3 counts to create the missing measures.

LESSON 2

1) Write in the counts under each measure. (Watch the time signature)

1   2-3-4   1   2   3-4   1-2   3-4   1-2-3-4

2) Write in the counts under each measure. (Watch the time signature)

1-2-3   1-2   3   1   2   3

3) Write in the counts to this song (this song is this weeks practice song so let this be a theory be a guide in your practice)

1 2 3   1 2 3   1 2 3   1 2 3   1 2 3

4) Draw a note head, O , in the proper spot for the letter name designated. (If you see a letter repeated it means that there are two different locations for that note name... a line note and a space note. Use both your sayings to figure out both locations).

A E C F D B G E Middle C

5) In each measure, draw a note stepping UP the staff.

6) In each measure, draw a note stepping DOWN the staff.

LESSON 3

1) Write if the notes are stepping, skipping or staying the same.

STEP   SKIP   SAME   STEP   SKIP

STEP   SAME   SKIP   SKIP   SKIP

2) Draw a note skipping UP in each measure from the note that is drawn

3) Draw a note skipping DOWN in each measure from the note that is drawn

4) Write in the counts to this song (this song is this weeks practice song so let this be a theory be a guide in your practice)

1   2   3   1   2   3   1   2   3

1   2   3   1   2   3   1   2   3   1   2-3

LESSON 4

1) Write step or skip in between each note.

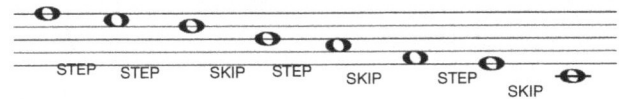

STEP STEP SKIP STEP SKIP STEP SKIP

2) Write step or skip or same in between each note.

STEP SKIP SAME SKIP STEP SKIP SAME STEP

3) Write step or skip in between

each note

STEP STEP SKIP STEP SKIP STEP SKIP

4) Write in the counts to this song (this song is this weeks practice song so let this be a theory be a guide in your practice)

1 2 3 1 2 3 1 2 3 1 2 3 1 2 3 1 2 3

1 2 3 1 2 3 1 2 3 1 2 3

5) Matching:

Repeat

Quarter note

Half note

Whole note

Slur

Forte

Piano

Dotted half note

Mezzo Forte

Grand staff

LESSON 5

1) Write step or skip or same in between each note.

STEP   SKIP   SAME   SKIP   STEP   SKIP   SAME   STEP

2) Circle all examples below that show a step on the piano.

3) Circle all examples below that show a skip on the piano

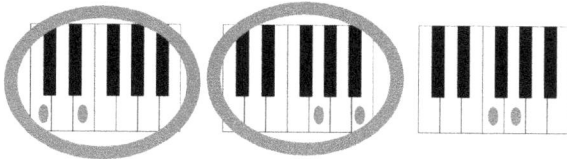

4) Write in the counts to this song (this song is this weeks practice song so let this be a theory be a guide in your practice)

1 2 3-4 | 1 2 3-4 | 1-2-3-4 | 1234 | 1-2 3-4

LESSON 6

1) In each measure, draw a note stepping UP the staff

2) In each measure, draw a note stepping DOWN the staff.

3) Just like in your flashcard practice, look at the images below and write the note name underneath them.

B   E   A   C   F   B

C   G   D   G   A

4) Add these note values together. When added how many total beats do they receive?

$$\text{♩} + \text{♩} = 3 \qquad \text{♩.} + \text{♩} = 5$$

$$\text{♩.} + \text{o} = 7 \qquad \text{o} + \text{♩} = 5$$

$$\text{o} + \text{♩} = 6 \qquad \text{♩} + \text{♩} = 4$$

$$\text{♩.} + \text{♩} = 4 \qquad \text{♩.} + \text{♩.} = 6$$

4) Write in the counts to this song (this song is this weeks practice song so let this be a theory be a guide in your practice)

1   2   3 | 1   2   3 | 1   2   3 | 1   2   3

1 - 2   3 | 1 - 2   3 | 1 - 2 - 3 | 1 - 2   3

1 - 2   3 | 1 - 2 - 3 | 1 - 2   3 | 1 - 2 - 3

Chapter 6 - FINDING ON THE PIANO THE NOTES ON THE STAFF

LESSON 1

1) Write in the counts and the missing bar line for the rhythm below

2) write in the number for how many beats you would hold the tied note for:

3) Write in the counts for the rhythm below. Then draw a star under where the claps will go when counting aloud. Then clap and count it aloud.

4). Write in the counts to this song (this song is this weeks practice song so let this be a theory be a guide in your practice)

5) Just like in your flashcard practice, look at the images below and write the note name underneath them.

E   F   D   C   G   C

D   B   A   F   E

LESSON 2

1) Write in the counts for the rhythm below. Then draw a star under where the claps will go when counting aloud. Then clap and count it aloud.

2) Write if the notes are located in the bass, middle or treble section of the piano

TREBLE   BASS

BASS   TREBLE

MIDDLE   MIDDLE

3) Write in the counts to this song (this song is this weeks practice song so let this be a theory be a guide in your practice)

4) In each measure, draw a note stepping UP the staff.

5) In each measure, draw a note stepping DOWN the staff.

LESSON 3

1) Write S for slur and T for Tie above each curved line to identify which are slurs and which are ties.

2) Write in the counts to this song (this song is this weeks practice song so let this be a theory be a guide in your practice

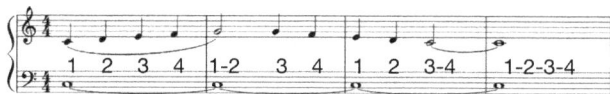

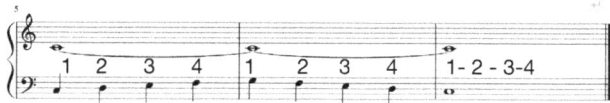

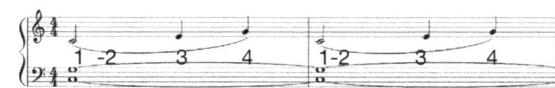

3) Write S below the curved lines that are Slurs and T   below the curved lines that are ties.

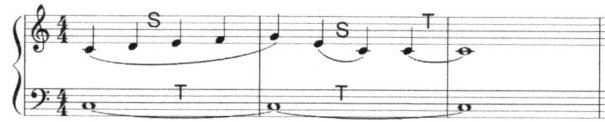

4) Draw a star on the note where the tunnel happens and 3rd finger hopping over happens in both hands going up and going down. Make sure to play it on your piano after you have written it down

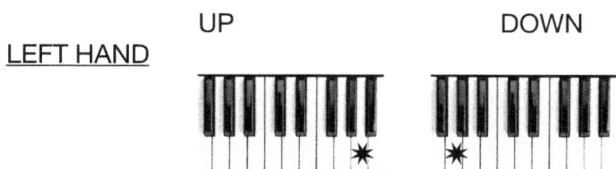

LESSON 4

1). Write S below the curved lines that are Slurs and T below the curved lines that are ties.

2) Write under each note if the note is located in the bass (B), middle (M) or treble (T) section of the piano.

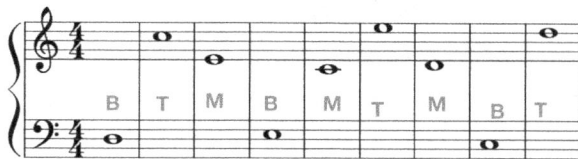

3). Write S below the curved lines that are Slurs and T below the curved lines that are ties.

4). Write in the counts to this song (this song is this weeks practice song so let this be a theory be a guide in your practice)

Chapter 7 - THE QUARTER REST

LESSON 1

1) Write under each note if the note is located in the bass (B), middle (M) or treble (T) section of the piano.

B T M B M T M B T

2) Just like in your flashcard practice, look at the images below and write the note name underneath them.

E   F   D   C   G   C

D   B   A   F   E

3) Draw circle note heads starting from middle C and going up 1 additional STEPS (C-D)

3) write in the number for how many beats you would hold the tied note for

= 2   = 3
= 4   = 6
= 6   = 4
= 8   = 5

4). Just like in your flashcard practice, look at the images below and write the note name underneath them.

B   E   A   C   F   B

C   G   D   G   A

5)Write in the counts to this song (this song is this weeks practice song so let this be a theory be a guide in your practice)

1-2 3 4 1-2 3 4 1-2 3 4 1-2 3 4

1   2 3 4 1 2 3 4 1-2-3-4

LESSON 2

1) is the example below 3/4 time or 4/4 time?
   __3/4_____

2) is the example below 3/4 time or 4/4 time?
   ___3/4_____

3) is the example below 3/4 time or 4/4 time?
   ___4/4_____

4) is the example below 3/4 time or 4/4 time?
   ___4/4_____

5) write in counts underneath.

6) Draw circle note heads starting from middle C and going up 3 additional STEPS (C-D-E)

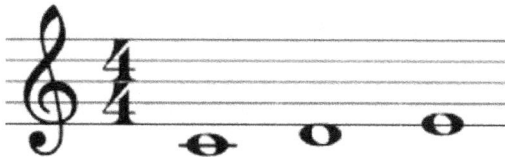

7) Write in the counts to this song (this song is this weeks practice song so let this be a theory be a guide in your practice)

LESSON 3

1) Write in the counts under neath the rhythm below. Then add a star under each spot that receives a clap. Then clap and count this rhythm aloud.

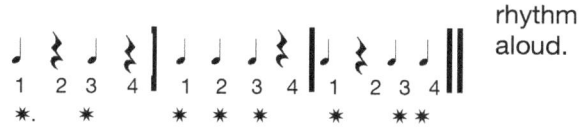

2) Draw in the notes below. note: All C's refer to bass c and not middle C. Answers may vary on notes that have 2 locations

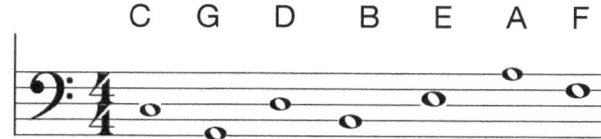

C   G   D   B   E   A   F

3) Draw in the notes below. note: All C's refer to treble c and not middle C. Answers may vary on notes have 2 locations.

C G D B E A F

4) Write in the counts under neath the rhythm below. Then add a star under each spot that receives a clap. Then clap and count this rhythm aloud. Then play the rhythm on a middle C note with the right hand 1 finger.

5) Write in the counts to this song (this song is this weeks practice song so let this be a theory be a guide in your practice)

6) Draw circle note heads starting from middle C and going up 4 additional STEPS (C-D-E-F)

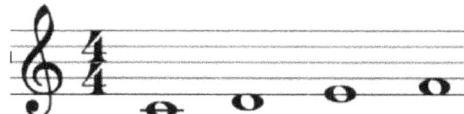

LESSON 4

1)   Write in the counts under neath the rhythm below. Then add a star under each spot that receives a clap. Then clap and count this rhythm aloud. Then play the rhythm on the correct notes

2) Draw circle note heads starting from middle C and going up 5 additional STEPS (C-D-E-F-G)

3) Write in the counts to this song (this song is this weeks practice song so let this be a theory be a guide in your practice)

LESSON 5

1) Draw circle note heads starting from middle C

and going up 6 additional STEPS (C-D-E-F-G -A)

2) Draw a quarter r _____

3) Draw a half note __

4) Draw a whole note _____

5) Draw a quarter rest ____

6) Draw a dotted half note _____

7) Write in the counts to this song (this song is this weeks practice song so let this be a theory be a guide in your practice)

Chapter 8: STACCATOS AND ACCIDENTALS

LESSON 1

1) Draw the note that gets 1 beat

2). Draw the note that gets 4 beats

3) Draw the note that gets 3 beats

4) Draw the note that gets 2 beats

5) Draw the rest that gets 1 beat

6) Draw circle note heads starting from middle C and going up 7 additional STEPS (C-D-E-F-G -A - B)

7) Write in the counts under neath the rhythm below. Then add a star under each spot that receives a clap. Then clap and count this rhythm aloud. Then play the rhythm on the correct notes

8) Write in the counts to this song (this song is this weeks practice song so let this be a theory be a guide in your practice)

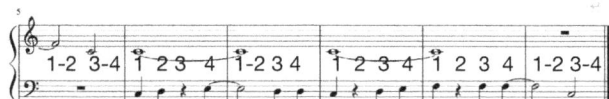

9) Write in the name of the note below each note that is drawn.

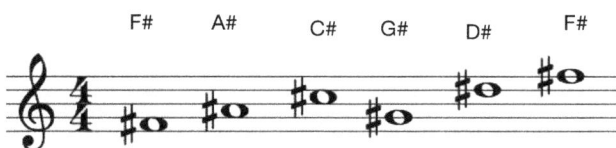

LESSON 2

1) Draw circle note heads starting from middle C and going up 8 additional STEPS (C-D-E-F-G -A - B - C) You have just drawn the C scale going up

2) Now that you can draw your C scale going up, you can draw it going down as well. On the staff below, start at treble C (the note you ended on on problem #1 above). Then step down 8 steps until you reach middle C. This is drawing the C scale going down.

3) Write in the name of the note below each note drawn.

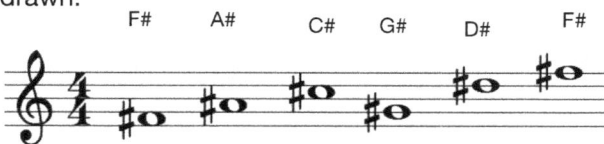

4) Write in the name of the note below each note that is drawn.

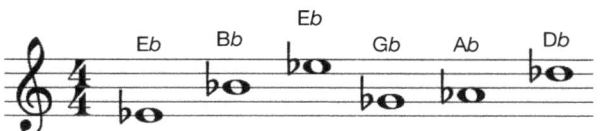

5) Circle a C #

6) Circle a Bb

7) Circle a F#

8) Circle a Db

9) Write in the counts to this song (this song is this weeks practice song so let this be a theory be a guide in your practice)

LESSON 3

1) Circle a D #

2) Circle a Eb

3) Circle a G#

4) Circle a Ab

5) Draw a C Scale going up on the first staff and a C scale going down on the second staff.

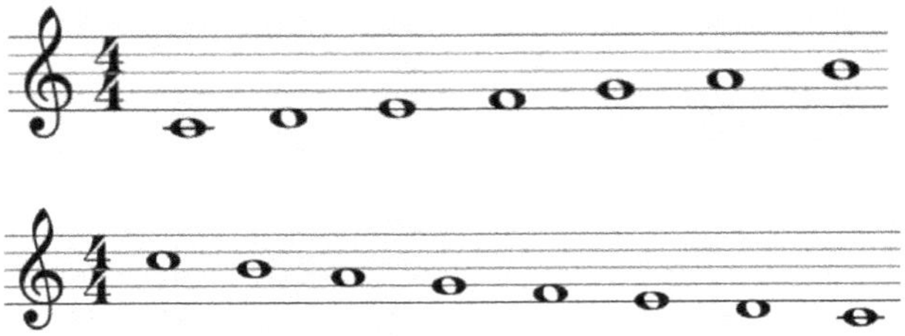

6) Write in the counts to this song (this song is this weeks practice song so let this be a theory be a guide in your practice)

LESSON 4

1) Matching:

2) Write in the counts to this song (this song is this weeks practice song so let this be a theory be a guide in your practice)

3) Draw a C scale going up then down on the same staff

4) Write in the name of the note below each note drawn.

F#   A#   C#   G#   D#   F#

5) Write in the name of the note below each note

Eb   Bb   Eb   Gb   Ab   Db

6) Draw the note that gets 1 beat ___

7). Draw the note that gets 4 beats ___

8) Draw the note that gets 3 beats _____

9) Draw the note that gets 2 beats _____

10) Draw the rest that gets 1 beat ___

11) Draw a quarter note _____

12) Draw a half note ___

13) Draw a whole note _____

14) Draw a quarter rest _____

15) Draw a dotted half note _____

16) Draw in the notes below. note: All C's refer to bass c and not middle C. Answers may vary on notes that have two locations on the staff.

C   G   D   B   E   A   F

17) Draw in the notes below. note: All C's refer to treble c and not middle C. Answers may vary on notes that have two locations on the staff

C   G   D   B   E   A   F

ABOUT THE AUTHOR:

Stephanie Parker has played classical piano for over 35 years. She attended Florida State University College of Music with a concentration in piano. She has been teaching piano for over 20 years as well as been a homeschooling mom since 2006. Homeschooling her children has given her a unique skill set to learn how to teach effectively mainly age ranges with many differing abilities. It has also shown her parents are very capable of teaching their children many subjects with the proper help which is why she wants to create this book to help parents who want to give the gift of music to their child, but may not have the time or money to do so.

www.ingramcontent.com/pod-product-compliance
Lightning Source LLC
Chambersburg PA
CBHW081240020426
42331CB00013B/3237